For that menagerie of marvels – where many magical Sunday afternoons
were spent – The Museum of Natural History in Oxford. And in memory
of biology teacher extraordinaire, Mr Tim Potts.

JC

To Zhanna, my wonderful mum,
who always supports and believes in me.

AK

LiTTLE TiGER
LONDON

CATERPILLAR BOOKS
An imprint of the Little Tiger Group
1 Coda Studios, 189 Munster Road, London SW6 6AW
Imported into the EEA by Penguin Random House Ireland,
Morrison Chambers, 32 Nassau Street, Dublin D02 YH68
www.littletiger.co.uk • First published in Great Britain 2021
Text copyright © James Carter 2021
Illustrations copyright © Alisa Kosareva 2021
A CIP catalogue record for this book
is available from the British Library
All rights reserved • ISBN: 978-1-83891-180-5
Printed in China • CPB/1400/1684/0321
2 4 6 8 10 9 7 5 3 1

THE BEASTS BENEATH OUR FEET

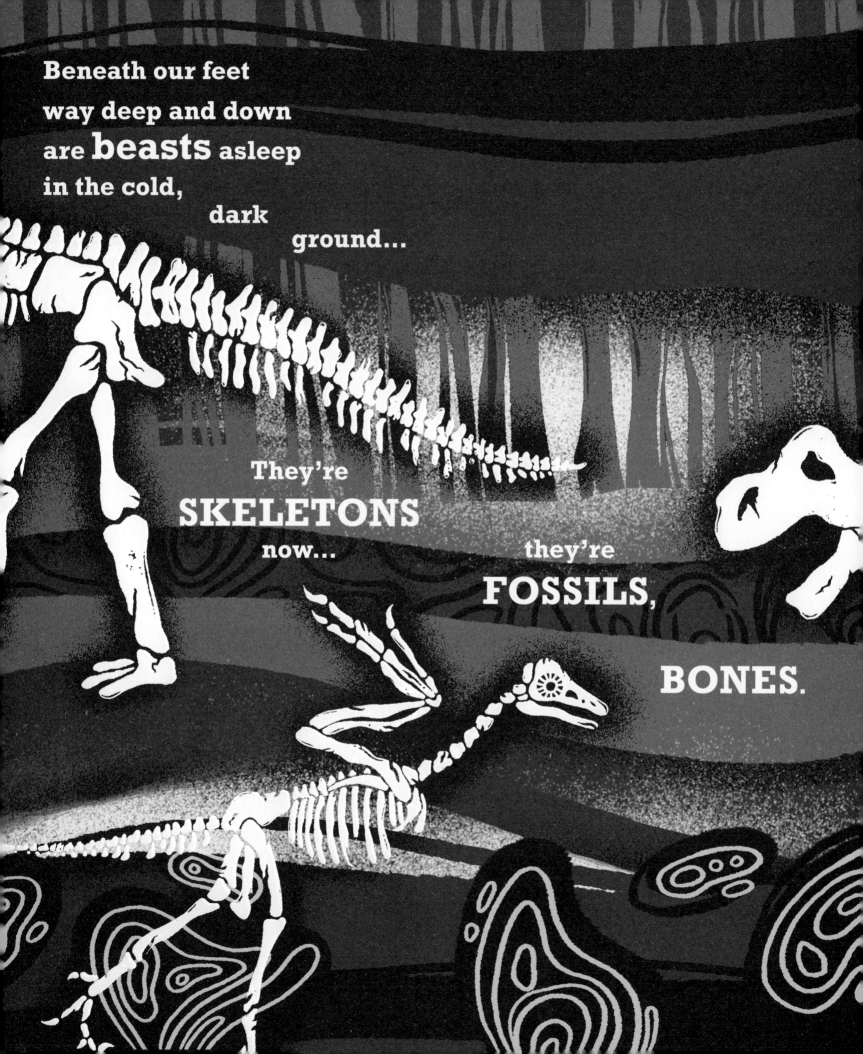

Beneath our feet
way deep and down
are **beasts** asleep
in the cold,
dark
ground...

They're
SKELETONS
now...

they're
FOSSILS,

BONES.

They're **silent**, still;
in a prison of stone.

So let's go see them
live their lives

and let's dig deep
through **ANCIENT TIMES.**

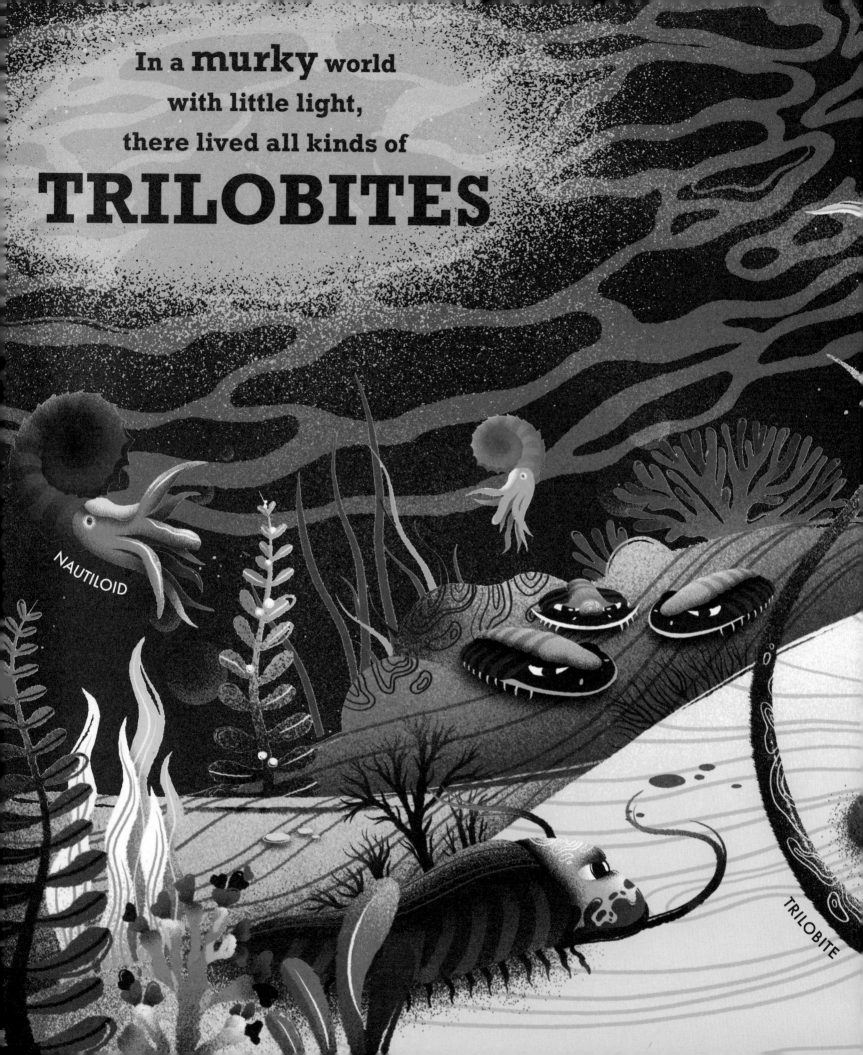

In a **murky** world
with little light,
there lived all kinds of
TRILOBITES

NAUTILOID

TRILOBITE

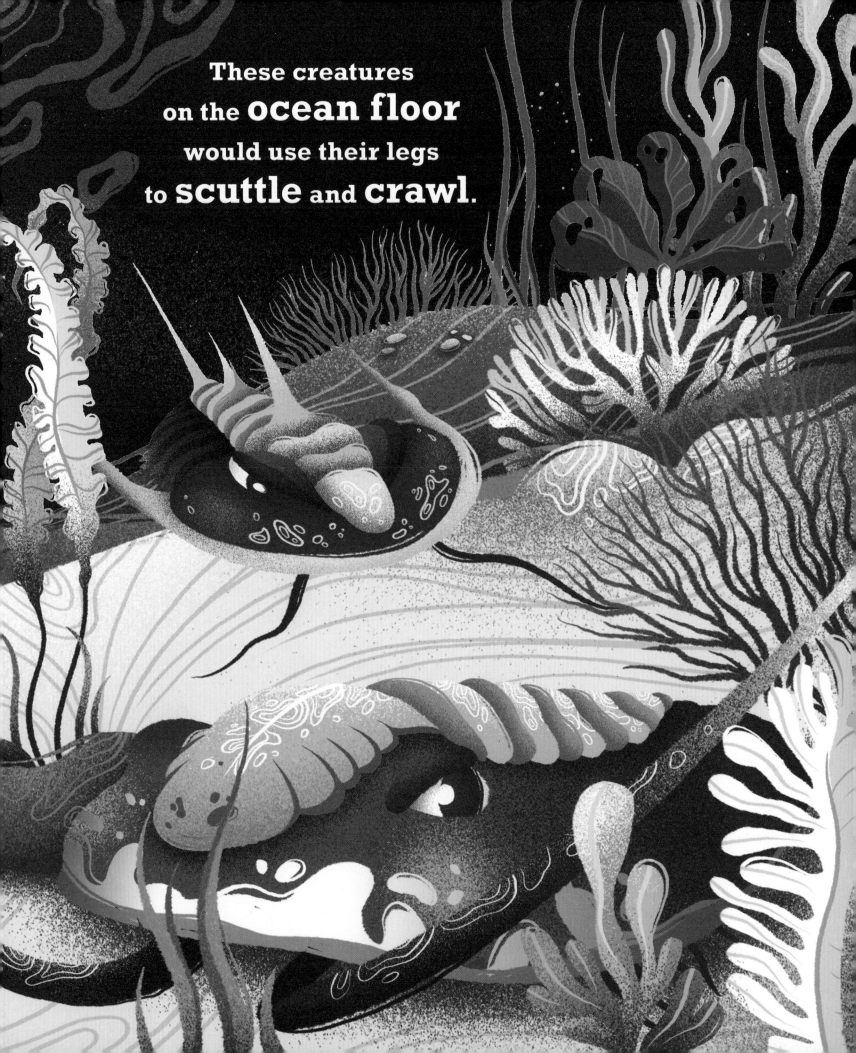

These creatures
on the **ocean floor**
would use their legs
to **scuttle** and **crawl**.

METOPOSAURUS,

built to swim,

**with four stubby,
stumpy
limbs.**

It fed on fish,
this **croc-like** beast,

with those **mighty,**
pointy teeth.

METOPOSAURUS

The **biggest bug**
there ever was

would **BUZZ** about

the ancient swamps.

MEGANEUROPSIS PERMIANA

COCKROACH

MEGANEUROPSIS
soared through sky –

an early
giant dragonfly.

A tiny head,
a neck so long,

its **whip-like** tail
went on and on.

ALLOSAURUS

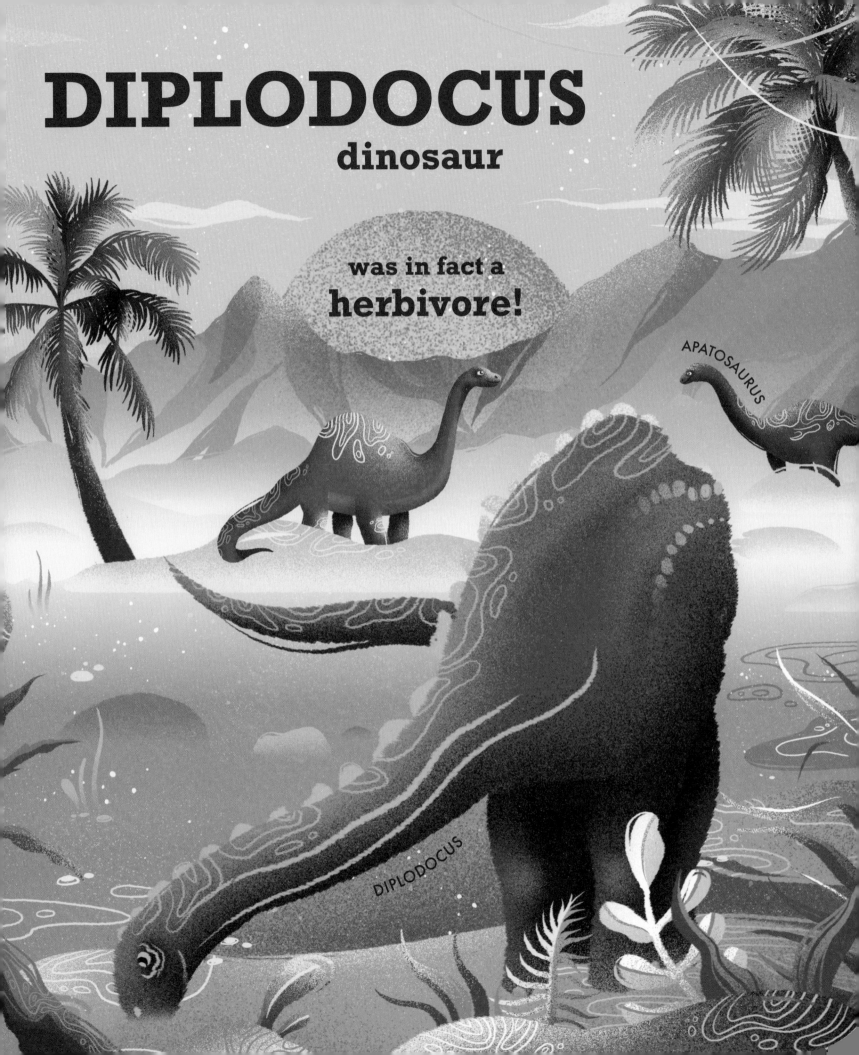

Which early,
quirky
bird was this?
The flashy
ARCHAEOPTERYX.

COMPSOGNATHUS

ARCHAEOPTERYX

With **feathered** wings
and **fancy** tail,
we think it flew
but **who can tell?**

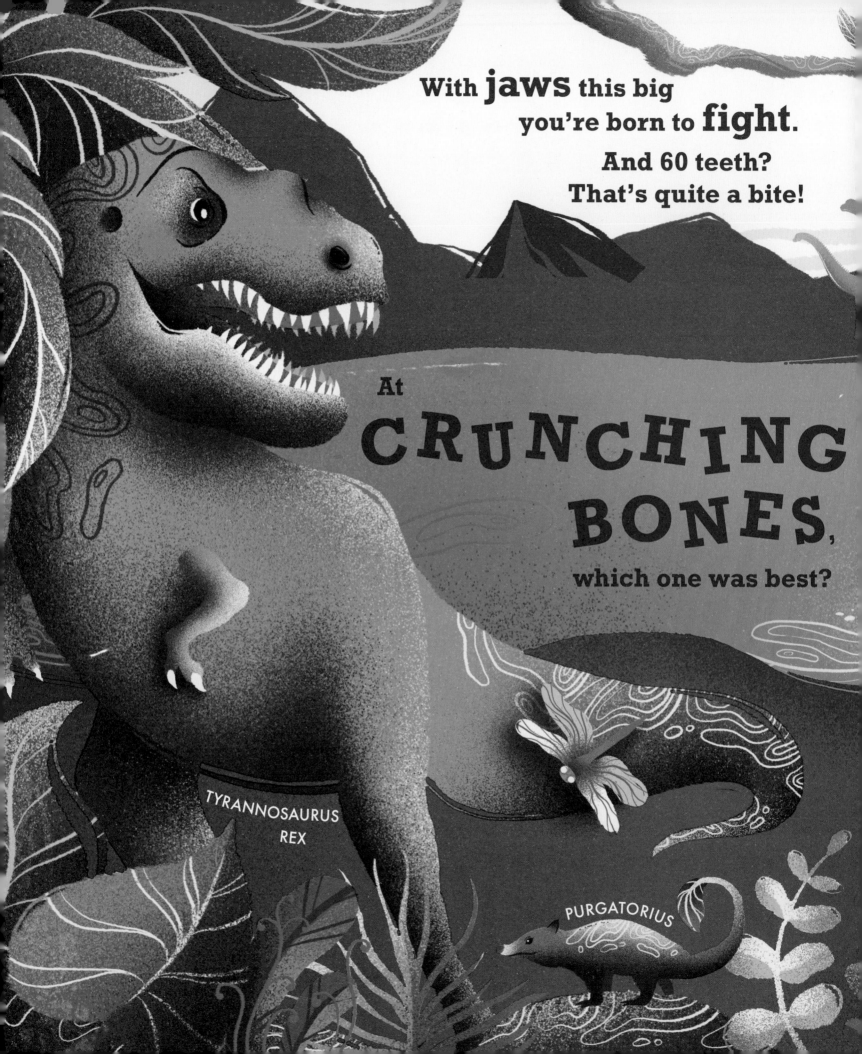

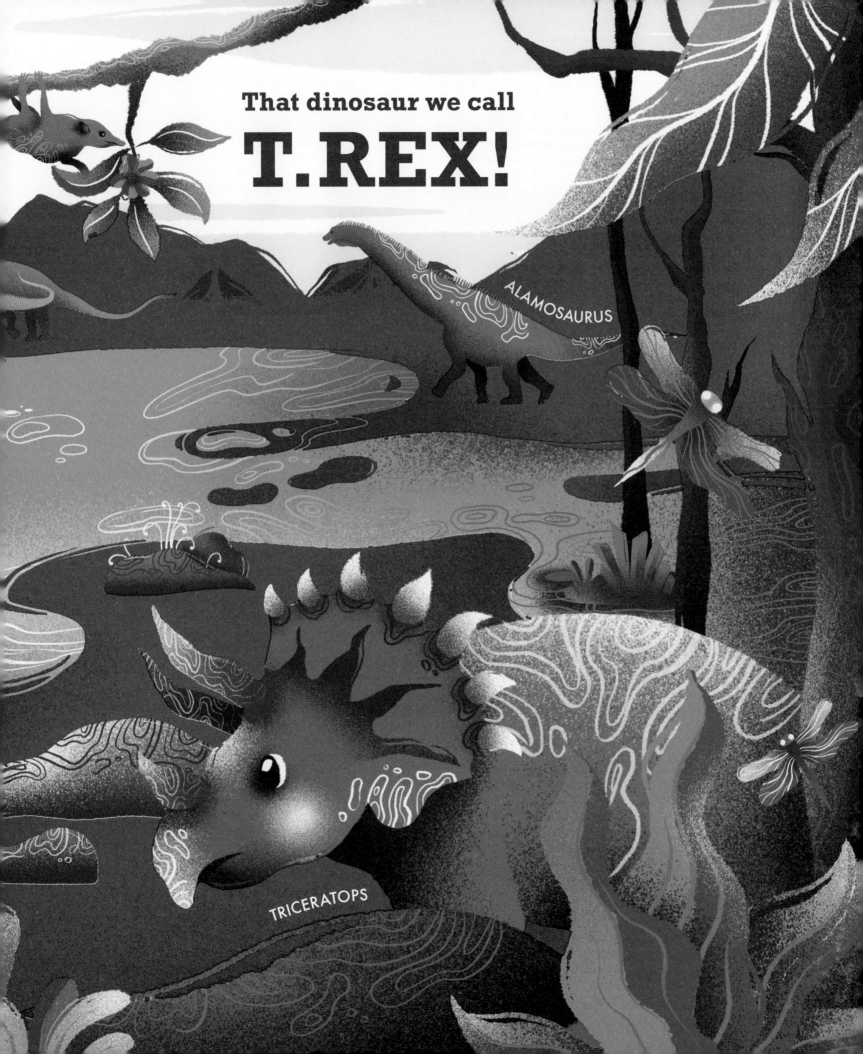

That dinosaur we call
T. REX!

ALAMOSAURUS

TRICERATOPS

In **northlands** lost
to fields of snow,
when **winter** came
and wouldn't go,

WOOLLY RHINO

with coats so thick
to beat the cold,

WOOLLY MAMMOTH

herds of **woolly mammoths** roamed.

vast volcanoes'
poisonous lavas –
lives were lost
to great disasters.

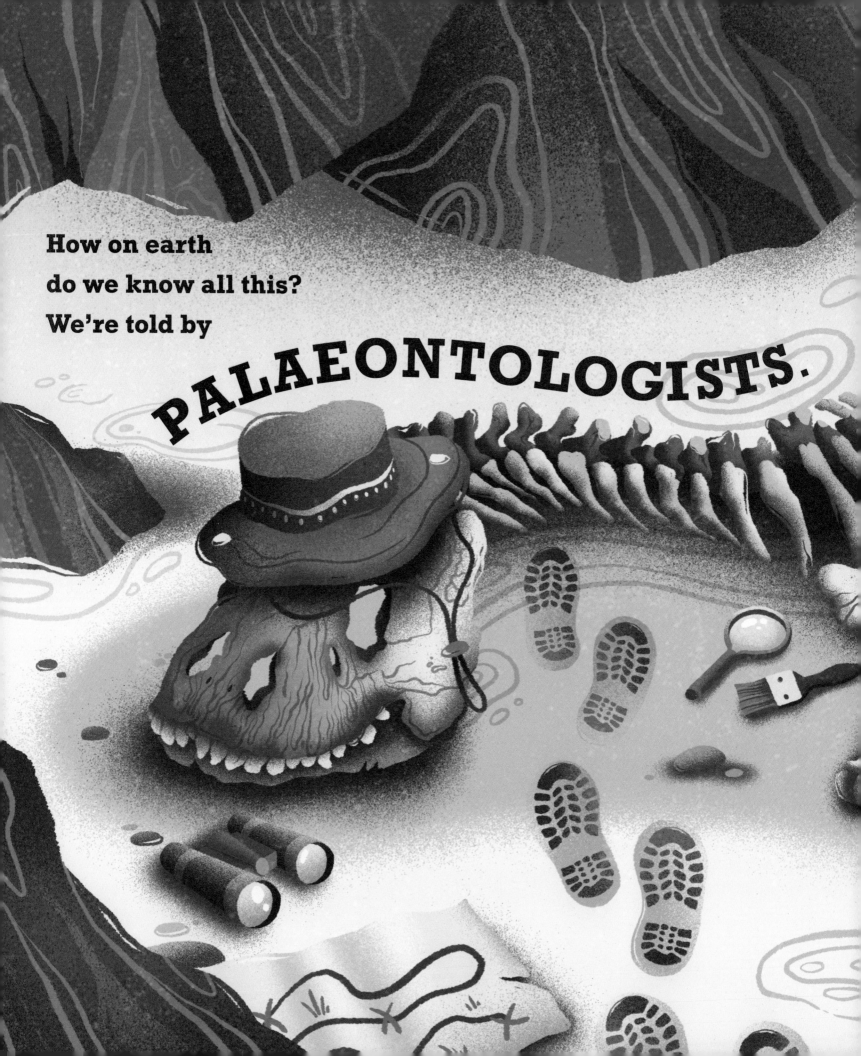

How on earth
do we know all this?
We're told by
PALAEONTOLOGISTS.

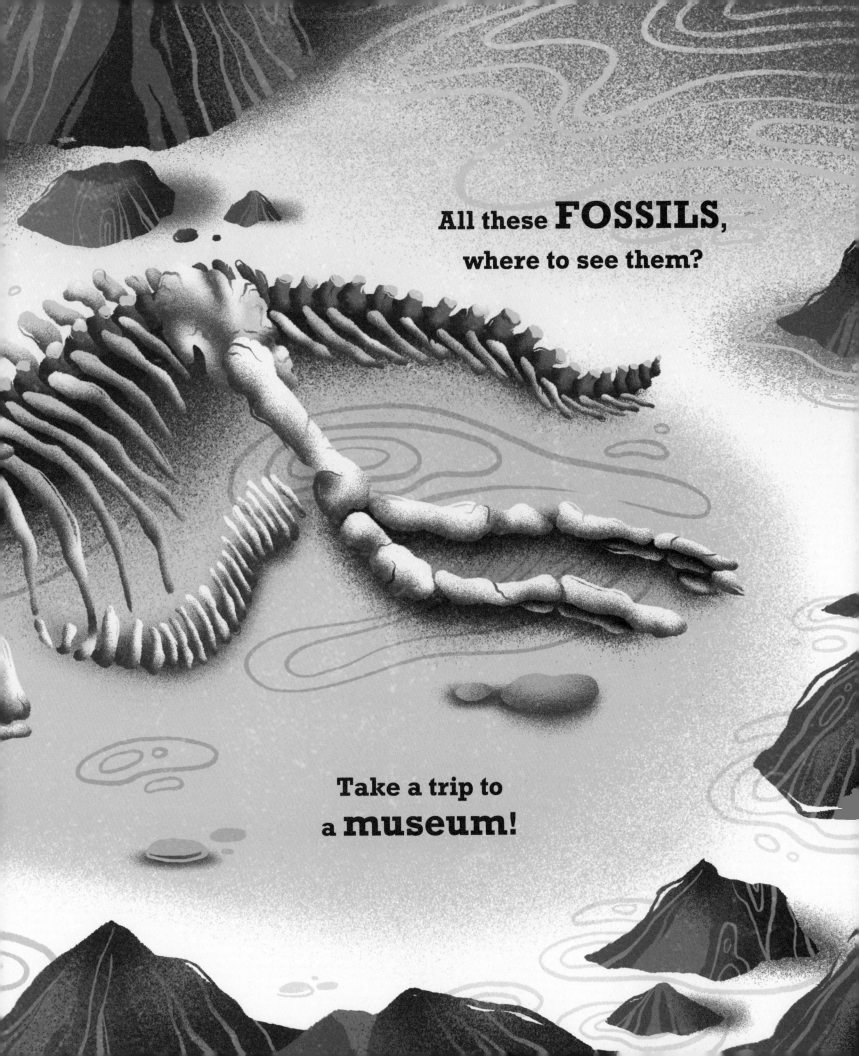

All these **FOSSILS**,
where to see them?

Take a trip to
a **museum!**

You too could find an

ancient beast.

Go grab a spade, dig

d
o
w
n

dig deep!

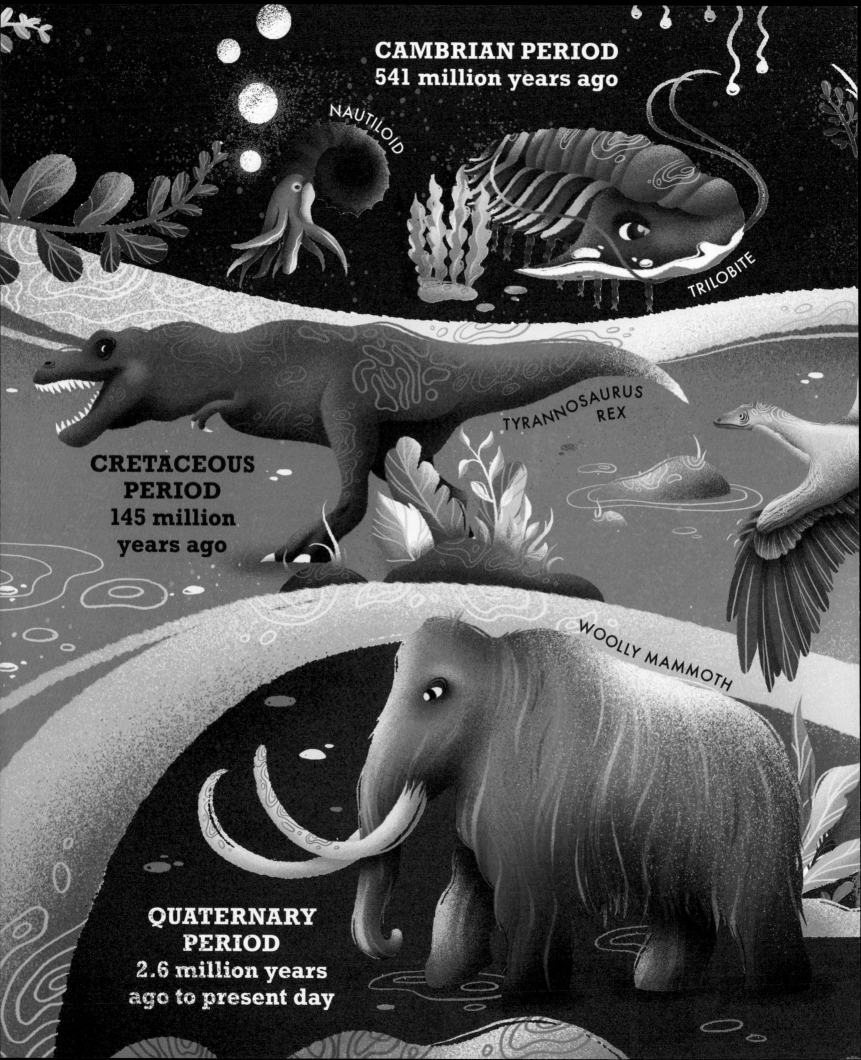